Seeing Things God's Way

DANIEL

BY BRYSON SMITH

Seeing Things God's Way
Pathway Bible Guides: Daniel
© Matthias Media 2007

Matthias Media
(St Matthias Press Ltd. ACN 067 558 365)
PO Box 225
Kingsford NSW 2032
Australia
Telephone: (02) 9663 1478; international: +61-2-9663-1478
Facsimile: (02) 9663 3265; international: +61-2-9663-3265
Email: info@matthiasmedia.com.au
Internet: www.matthiasmedia.com.au

ISBN 978 1 921068 68 3

Cover design and typesetting by Lankshear Design Pty Ltd.

CONTENTS

Before you begin 5

1: Courage (Daniel 1) 7

2: Wisdom (Daniel 2) 11

3: Salvation (Daniel 3 & 6) 15

4: Humility (Daniel 4-5) 19

5: Dominion (Daniel 7) 23

6: Endurance (Daniel 8) 27

7: Forgiveness (Daniel 9) 31

8: Hope (Daniel 10-12) 37

For the leader 45

BEFORE YOU BEGIN

Sometimes things are not what they seem. Sometimes things that seem important turn out to be unimportant. Sometimes things that seem permanent turn out to be temporary. Sometimes things that seem valuable turn out to be worthless.

That's why Daniel is such an important book. It powerfully reminds us to always see things God's way. At the heart of the story is a young man named Daniel, far from home, forced to study the learning and wisdom of the empire that had gutted his own, destroying the temple of his God and killing many of his countrymen.

Behind this story lies a greater reality. The powerful kingdom of the Babylonians will not last, and even the powerful kingdom that replaces it will be torn down to be replaced by more temporary dynasties. One king, however, rules over all. The Lord of Israel uses the story of Daniel to point towards an eternal kingdom that reveals the power of his Son Jesus.

Any Christian who picks up the book of Daniel will find much to sympathize with. Political power and social pressure will push us around, and challenge our faith, in ways that we don't expect. Where are we going to find encouragement? In Daniel's God—the same God that rules over the kings of the ancient world is the God who rules today through the king he's appointed—Jesus Christ.

To get the most out of this Pathway Guide to Daniel, please read the whole of Daniel at least once before you get started on the studies, and ask God to give you his wisdom to live the message that's in the book.

Bryson Smith
March 2007

1. COURAGE

Daniel 1

 ## Getting started

If the Christian life is hard, what comfort does Jesus give us? Consider Jesus' words: "In the world you will have tribulation. But take heart; I have overcome the world" (John 16:33).

⚡ Light from the Word

Read Daniel 1:1-2.

1. What historical events are described at the very beginning of Daniel?

2. The events of verses 1-2 are often referred to as 'the Exile'. Lamentations is another Old Testament book written about this same event. Skim through Lamentations 1. What effect did the Exile have on Israel?

Read Daniel 1:3-7.

3. As well as carrying back treasure to Babylon, Nebuchadnezzar also carried back people! What did this involve for people like Daniel?

4. How do you think Daniel may have felt about all the changes being forced upon him?

5. How is Daniel's experience like ours?

Read Daniel 1:8-20.

6. Why do you think Daniel refuses to eat the king's food?

7. Compare what the royal official expects to happen to Daniel (v. 10) with what actually happens (v. 15). What do you think is the lesson of this incident?

8. This chapter describes a time of trouble and trials for God's people. What evidence do you find in the chapter that God is still in control?

 ## To finish

What are some areas of life in which you are tempted to compromise on your obedience to Jesus? In what way is this chapter a good encouragement to us?

 ## Give thanks and pray

Give thanks to God for his promise that nothing can separate us from his love (Rom 8:37-39). Pray that we won't compromise in the areas mentioned in the previous question.

2. WISDOM

Daniel 2

 Getting started

Do you know anyone who you would describe as wise? What is it about them that makes them wise?

🔆 Light from the Word

Read Daniel 2:1-13.

1. What effect does Nebuchadnezzar's dream have on him?

2. Why does Nebuchadnezzar refuse to tell the wise men his dream?

Read Daniel 2:14-30.

3. What effect does Nebuchadnezzar's dream have on Daniel?

4. List all the things we discover about God in these verses.

Read Daniel 2:31-45.

5. Describe Nebuchadnezzar's dream and Daniel's interpretation in your own words.

6. Daniel tells Nebuchadnezzar that the Babylonian Empire is represented by the gold head in the dream. Why do you think he doesn't identify the other kingdoms represented in the dream (vv. 39-43)?

7. What do you think is the most important kingdom in Nebuchadnezzar's dream? Why?

Read Daniel 2:46-49.

8. What does Nebuchadnezzar come to realize about God?

9. Look back over the chapter and notice how many times "wise men" or "wisdom" have been mentioned. What do you think this chapter is telling us about wisdom?

 ## To finish

If we really believe what Daniel says about God in verses 20-23, how will it show in the way we live?

 ## Give thanks and pray

Re-read Daniel 2:20-23 and use it as a basis for thanks and prayer.

3. SALVATION

Daniel 3 & 6

 **Getting started**

In what situations do you feel like the 'odd one out' for being a Christian?

 **Light from the Word**

In this study we will be reading two chapters in which quite similar things happen. Read Daniel 3 and 6 and fill in the following chart.

	Daniel 3	Daniel 6
Who is the king at the time of this chapter?		
What does the king command?		
Which followers of God are focused on in these chapters?		
How do these followers of God respond to the king's command?		
What punishment do the followers of God face?		

	Daniel 3	Daniel 6
How are the followers of God rescued?		
How does each rescue highlight that it is God who is saving his people?		
What does the king eventually decide about the God of Israel?		

1. "Regardless of the particular empire, the particular king or even the particular type of ruler in power, God's people will inevitably face opposition." How do Daniel 3 and 6 illustrate this statement?

2. In chapter 3, the king's command is for people to do something, whereas in chapter 6, the king's command is for people to *not* do something. What are some of the varied ways in which our present world opposes God's people?

Read Hebrews 11:32-12:3.

3. Shadrach, Meshach, Abednego and Daniel all showed great faith—a faith that is perfected in Christ. How should this be an encouragement to us?

 ## To finish

In what ways do you feel the opposition of the world in your own Christian life? What things help you to remain firm?

 ## Give thanks and pray

Pray for our Christian brothers and sisters around the world who are facing fierce and violent persecution for their faith. Pray that they would persevere to the end, and thank God for his promise that our present sufferings are not worth comparing with the glory that will be revealed to us (Rom 8:18).

4. HUMILITY

Daniel 4-5

 Getting started

"Pride goes before a fall." Do you agree? Can you think of any examples from your own experience, or from observation, when this has happened?

☀ Light from the Word

In this study we will again read two chapters that are very closely linked.

Read Daniel 4.

1. What is it that prompts Nebuchadnezzar's pride (vv. 29-30)?

2. Why is Nebuchadnezzar's pride especially disappointing given:

    a. the dream he had in 4:1-27?

    b. what he had already learnt in chapters 2 and 3?

3. How is Nebuchadnezzar humbled by God?

4. What does Nebuchadnezzar come to realize about God (4:1-3, 34-37)?

Read Daniel 5.

5. In what way is King Belshazzar's pride even worse than his father's?

6. How is King Belshazzar humbled by God?

7. What do you think the main lesson of these two chapters is?

8. How would these chapters have been a comfort to God's people (especially at the time of Daniel)?

9. How are these chapters a challenge to God's people?

10. 1 Peter 2:22-23 describes Christ suffering for us and leaving us an example to follow. In what ways does Jesus exemplify the lesson of these two chapters in Daniel?

 ## To finish

Are there any areas of life in which you are especially prone to pride? What are ways in which we can encourage humility in each other?

Give thanks and pray

Think about the examples of pride in these chapters. Thank God that he has delivered us from sin in Jesus, and pray that he would continue to deliver us and make us humble.

5. DOMINION

Daniel 7

 **Getting started**

What were the most important things you did last week?

💡 Light from the Word

Read Daniel 7:1.

1. How is this chapter different from any of the previous chapters?

Read Daniel 7:2-14.

2. Daniel's dream has three scenes. Describe the main thing that happens in each scene.

- Scene 1 (vv. 2-8)

- Scene 2 (vv. 9-12)

- Scene 3 (vv. 13-14)

Note: The phrase "son of man" refers to a human being (i.e. someone who is a member of mankind). For this reason Daniel himself is referred to as a "son of man" in 8:17.

Read Daniel 7:15-28.

3. What do the four beasts represent?

Note: Many people spend lots of time trying to figure out what specific kingdoms are represented by the four beasts. A common explanation is that they represent the Babylonian, Persian, Greek and Roman Empires. According to this interpretation, the boastful horn of the fourth beast corresponds to Antiochus Epiphanes, a particularly vicious persecutor of God's people. Whether this interpretation is true or not, the chapter doesn't explicitly say. Rather, the main focus of the chapter is not on the beasts but on the "one like a son of man".

4. Who does the "one like a son of man" represent (vv. 18, 26-7)?

5. How is the lesson of Daniel's vision a comfort for God's people?

6. When we turn to the New Testament, Jesus does something very exciting with this chapter. According to Jesus, who is the Son of Man (Mark 14:60-62)?

7. In the light of your previous answer, what does Daniel's vision tell us about the majesty and importance of Jesus?

8. In what ways does this world tempt us to underestimate the importance of Jesus?

 ## To finish

Considering what we have discovered in Daniel 7, what would God say were the most important things we did last week? How does this compare to your answer to the 'Getting started' question?

 ## Give thanks and pray

Jesus' dominion is "an everlasting dominion, which shall not pass away, and his kingdom one that shall not be destroyed". Ask God to help you live in light of this.

6. ENDURANCE

Daniel 8

 Getting started

"I'm thinking of giving up being a Christian. It's too hard because people just think you're strange!" What sorts of things might you say in response?

🔆 Light from the Word

Read Daniel 8:1-14.

1. How is the ram described in Daniel's dream?

2. How is the goat described in Daniel's dream?

3. What feelings and emotions does Daniel's dream evoke in you?

Read Daniel 8:15-27.

4. Who is the ram identified as?

5. Who is the goat identified as?

Historical note: Daniel's vision provides a good overview of the history of the Greek Empire. Under the leadership of Alexander the Great (v. 21), the Greek Empire grew in size and power. After Alexander's early death, however, the empire was divided amongst four of his generals (v. 22).

6. Considerable attention is especially given to one of the goat's horns (vv. 9-12, 23-25). Why do you think this particular horn is given so much attention?

Historical note: It is generally considered that the "king of bold face" (v. 23) is a reference to Antiochus Epiphanes. Epiphanes was a particularly vicious persecutor of God's people and, amongst other things, banned Sabbath-keeping and circumcision amongst the Israelites, violently punished those who disobeyed him, and set up sacrifices to his god in the Jerusalem temple.

7. Why do you think God is providing Daniel with this insight into the future?

8. How does the lesson of this vision build on the lesson of the previous chapter?

9. "In Daniel's vision we see that God is still in control even when things seem to be going wrong." How is this lesson also seen in the life, death and resurrection of Jesus Christ?

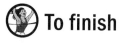 **To finish**

What things help you to persevere when you're being criticized for being a follower of Jesus?

 Give thanks and pray

As in Study 3, pray again for Christians in the world who are struggling against fierce persecution. Thank God that he will return to judge those who persecute Christians.

7. FORGIVENESS

Daniel 9

 Getting started

"God is just a grumpy old man ... always looking for things to get angry about!" How would you respond to a comment like that?

💡 Light from the Word

Read Daniel 9:1-3.

1. What is it that Daniel discovers from the prophet Jeremiah?

2. Jeremiah lived at the same time as Daniel. However, whereas Daniel was taken as an exile to Babylon (see Study 1), Jeremiah remained living amongst the ruins of Jerusalem. One of the things that Jeremiah did was write a letter to the exiles in Babylon. It is probably this letter which Daniel is reading in verse 2. Read the following extract from his letter:

> These are the words of the letter that Jeremiah the prophet sent from Jerusalem to the surviving elders of the exiles, and to the priests, the prophets, and all the people, whom Nebuchadnezzar had taken into exile from Jerusalem to Babylon ...
> "For thus says the LORD: When seventy years are completed for Babylon, I will visit you, and I will fulfill to you my promise and bring you back to this place. For I know the plans I have for you, declares the LORD, plans for wholeness and not for evil, to give you a future and a hope. Then you will call upon me and come and pray to me, and I will hear you. You will seek me and find me. When you seek me with all your heart, I will be found by you, declares the LORD, and I will restore your fortunes and gather you from all the nations and all the places where I have driven you, declares the LORD, and I will bring you back to the place from which I sent you into exile." (Jer 29:1, 10-14)

a. What does God promise to do?

b. When does God promise to do it?

3. The first year of Darius (v. 1) places this chapter about 65-70 years after the start of the Exile—when the Persian Empire had conquered the Babylonians. Given your answers to the previous two questions, how might Daniel be feeling at this time? What does Daniel do in response (v. 3)?

Read Daniel 9:4-19.

4. According to Daniel, why did the Exile happen?

5. What does Daniel ask God to do?

6. On what basis does he ask God to do this?

7. Is Daniel's prayer an appropriate one for us all to pray? Why and in what way (or why not)?

Read Daniel 9:20-23.

8. In what ways do we see God's eagerness to forgive and answer prayer in these verses?

Read Daniel 9:24-27.

Note: These are quite difficult verses in which God gives Daniel an overview of his plan to provide "everlasting righteousness" for his people. Many people have used these verses to develop elaborate timelines for either the first appearance of Jesus or the return of Jesus. The verses, however, seem to be deliberately vague. Rather than giving a highly detailed plan to Daniel, God instead simply wants Daniel to know that a plan exists.

9. How does God's plan to "bring in everlasting righteousness" find its fulfillment? (Look up Rom 3:21-26, 4:22-25; 2 Cor 1:20.)

10. In Daniel 9 we see God's eagerness to forgive. How is this even more obvious at the cross of Christ (1 John 4:9-10)?

 ## To finish

At what times do you doubt God's goodness and generosity to you? How does this chapter help at those times?

 ## Give thanks and pray

Give thanks to God for his eagerness to show love and mercy to his people.

8. HOPE

Daniel 10-12

 Getting started

When do you find it hard to remain convinced that God is in control?

☀ Light from the Word

Read Daniel 10:1-11:1.

In this study we will cover a very complex vision that Daniel received. The vision will go right through until the end of the book. These are difficult chapters. A helpful summary of these chapters is provided in the Matthias Media Interactive Bible Study on Daniel, *Kingdom of Dreams*. This summary has been reproduced at the end of the study. For the purposes of this study, we'll be content just getting some of the main ideas and not worrying too much about the detail.

1. According to the man in Daniel's vision, what is the main theme of these chapters (10:1, 14)?

2. What attributes of Daniel's character are commended (10:12)? Can you think of any places in the book where we have seen these attributes?

Skim read Daniel 11:2-45 (it's very complex, so don't get too worried about all the details).

3. What human kingdoms does this chapter involve (11:2)?

4. The chapter is full of quite precise predictions of the political intrigue and struggle for power within the Greek Empire following Alexander the Great. This certainly happened in history, although it's hard to know exactly what is being referred to in some of the verses. What feelings and emotions does this chapter produce in you?

5. What are we repeatedly told through the vision (11:27, 29, 35)? In what way is this a comfort?

Read Daniel 12.

6. Again it's hard to determine exactly what these verses refer to. Some think it is another reference to the fierce persecution of God's people under Antiochus Epiphanes (see Study 6). Others think that the vision has now jumped forward to a future persecution that will happen just before the return of Jesus. Irrespective of these options, what is going to happen to God's people (12:2-3)?

7. What is going to happen to those who are not God's people?

8. Look back over your previous two answers. In what ways should those truths influence:

   • how we spend our time?

- how we spend our money?

- how we treat other Christians?

- how we treat people who don't yet know Jesus?

 To finish

Look back over the studies in this book. Daniel has helped us see the things of this world from God's perspective. Has there been any one particular truth that has especially impacted you? How has it helped you understand and value Jesus all the more?

 Give thanks and pray

Give thanks to God that he remains in control even when terrible and confusing things are happening in the world.

Dan 10:1-14	It is the third year of Cyrus, King of Persia, and Daniel is deep in prayer. In response to his prayers, God sends a messenger to instruct him and to outline for him future history.
Dan 11:2-4	The Persian kings of Daniel's time will be overthrown by a mighty Greek king, Alexander the Great (11:3). He will die early, leaving an empire to be divided among four generals. Two of the kingdoms which spring out of this division will become prominent—Egypt in the South and Syria in the North.
Dan 11:5-17	These two kingdoms will war against each other, attempt alliances and act treacherously with each other. There will even be a time of peace between them.
Dan 11:18-28	However, eventually a particular king in the North will be murdered and his natural successor will be prevented from coming to the throne by the quick action of a usurper, Antiochus Epiphanes IV. This contemptible person will depose the current Jewish High Priest and murder him, seizing rich lands and acquiring wealth. He will make two campaigns against Egypt and plot to destroy his nephew in the South.
	He will also resolve to destroy all those in Palestine who are loyal to the covenant God made with his people. To this end, he will stop at the Holy City, Jerusalem, on his way back from Egypt and enter the temple and plunder its sacred treasures.
Dan 11:29-30	His second campaign against Egypt in the South will bring him face to face with the Romans, who will stop him from waging war against Egypt. Fresh from this rebuff, he will decide to strengthen his rule at home through making his citizens fully Greek. This programme will start with dissident Jews who have given up the covenant made by God with Moses.

Dan 11:31-32	He will then act to stop the daily sacrifice in the temple, knowing that only faithful Jews will resist. They act as expected, resisting even under brutal persecution, pillaging, death and imprisonment. Nevertheless, persecution continues.
Dan 11:33-35	The faithful Jews are not rescued by divine intervention as Daniel and his friends had been, although they do receive a little help (perhaps through the encouragement of the first Judean guerillas and activists).
Dan 11:36-39	It is at this point that the picture painted by the angel becomes quite fuzzy and unclear to us. Like all those who step out from under the king of heaven's rule, this king will claim to be God, doing as he pleases. He will succeed, but only until God chooses to put an end to it.
Dan 11:40-12:3	Yet again the details become hard for us to understand. The messenger's telescopic lens focuses even more on the distant future, stating that there will be opposition and the falling of many nations. There will be an affront against the people of God and the land of God's people, a subsequent retreat, and the death of this one who sets himself against the King of heaven and against the people of the king of heaven.
	In this last great battle there will be many deaths. The godly and ungodly will alike die. Together they will sleep in the dust of the earth and together they will awake from sleep to judgement.
	The wise, who have feared God and turned many to right relationship with the God of heaven, will awake to everlasting life. They will shine like the stars for ever and ever.
	On the other hand, the godless, who have rejected the King of heaven, will wake to everlasting contempt and disgrace.

FOR THE LEADER

What are Pathway Bible Guides?

The Pathway Bible Guides aim to provide simple, straightforward Bible study material for:

- Christians who are new to studying the Bible (perhaps because they've been recently converted or because they have joined a Bible study group for the first time);
- Christians who find other studies[1] too much of a stretch.

Accordingly, we've designed the studies to be short, straightforward and easy to use, with a simple vocabulary. At the same time, we've tried to do justice to the passages being studied, and to model good Bible-reading principles. We've tried to be simple without being simplistic; no-nonsense without being no-content.

The questions and answers assume a small group context, but it should be easy to adapt them to suit different situations, such as individual study and one-to-one.

Your role as leader

Because many in your group may not be used to reading and discussing a Bible passage in a group context, a greater level of responsibility will fall to you as the leader of the discussions. There are the usual responsibilities of preparation, prayer and managing group dynamics. In addition, there will be an extra dimension of forming and encouraging good Bible reading habits in people who may not have much of an idea of what those habits look like.

Questions have been kept deliberately brief and simple. For this reason, you may have to fill in some of the gaps that may have been addressed in, say, an Interactive Bible Study. Such 'filling in' may take the form of asking follow-up questions, or using your best judgement to work out when you might need to

1. Such as the Interactive Bible Study (IBS) series also available from Matthias Media.

supply background information. That sort of information, and some suggestions about other questions you could ask, may be found in the following leader's notes. In addition, a *New Bible Dictionary* is always a useful aid to preparation, and simple commentaries such as those in the *Tyndale* or *Bible Speaks Today* series are often helpful. On Daniel, *Kingdoms in Conflict: Reading Daniel Today*[2] by Andrew Reid is excellent. Consult these resources after you have done your own preparation.

On the question of background information, these studies are written from the assumption that God's word stands alone. God works through his Holy Spirit and the leaders he has gifted—such as you—to make his meaning clear. Assuming this to be true, the best interpreter and provider of background information for Scripture will not be academic historical research, but Scripture itself. Extra historical information may be useful for the purpose of illustration, but it is unnecessary for understanding and applying what God says to us.

The format of the studies

The discussion questions on each passage follow a simple pattern. There is a question at the beginning of each discussion that is intended to get people talking around the issues raised by the passage, and to give you some idea of how people are thinking. If the group turns out to be confident, motivated and comfortable with each other and the task at hand, you may even decide to skip this question. Alternatively, if the group members are shy or quiet, you may decide to think of related types of questions that you could add in to the study, so as to maintain momentum in a non-threatening way.

After the first question, the remaining questions work through the passage sequentially, alternating between observation, interpretation and application in a way that will become obvious when you do your own preparation. The final question of each discussion, just before the opportunity for prayer, could be used in some groups to encourage (say) one person each week to give a short talk (it could be 1 minute or 5 minutes, depending on the topic and the people). The thinking here is that there's no better way to encourage understanding of a passage than to get people to the point where they can explain it to others. Use your judgement in making best use of this final exercise each week, depending on the people in your group.

. . . .

2. Andrew Reid, *Kingdoms in Conflict: Reading Daniel Today*, AIO, Sydney, 1993.

In an average group, it should be possible to work through the study in approximately 45 minutes. But it's important that you work out what your group is capable of, given the time available, and make adjustments accordingly. Work out in advance which questions or sub-points can be omitted if time is short. And have a few supplementary questions or discussion starters up your sleeve if your group is dealing with the material quickly and hungering for more. Each group is different. It's your job as leader to use the printed material as 'Bible *Guides*', and not as a set of questions that you must rigidly stick to regardless of your circumstances.

Preparation: 60/40/20

Ideally, group members should spend half an hour reading over the passage and pencilling in some answers *before* they come to the group. Not every group member will do this, of course, but encourage them with the idea that the more they prepare for the study, the more they will get out of the discussion.

In terms of your own preparation as leader, we recommend you put aside approximately *two hours*, either all at once or in two one-hour blocks, and that you divide up the time as follows:

- 60 minutes reading the passage and answering the questions yourself as best you can (without looking at the leader's notes or Bible commentaries);
- 40 minutes consulting the leader's notes (plus other resources, like commentaries). Add to your own answers, and jot down supplementary questions or other information that you want to have available as you lead the discussion. Make sure you write everything you need on the study pages—the last thing you want to do is to keep turning to the 'answers' in the back during the group discussion;
- 20 minutes praying about the study and for your group members.

This 60/40/20 pattern will help you to focus on the Bible and what it's saying, rather than simply regurgitating to the group what is in the leader's notes. Remember, these notes are just that—notes to offer some help and guidance. They are not the Bible! As a pattern of preparation, 60/40/20 also helps you to keep praying for yourself and your group, that God would give spiritual growth as his word is sown in your hearts (see Luke 8:4-15; 1 Cor 3:5-7).

If, for some reason, you have less or more time to spend in preparation, simply apply the 60/40/20 proportions accordingly.

1. COURAGE

Daniel 1

▶ Remember: 60/40/20

 Getting started

John 16:33 was spoken by Jesus to his disciples the night before he was crucified. Jesus explained to them that the world hated him, and that it will also hate his followers. The comfort, however, is that Jesus had overcome the world by not giving in to the world. In humble submission to the Father, Jesus was obedient even to death on a cross. In so doing, Jesus has established a kingdom of forgiveness and salvation for his people. It's a kingdom that will last forever.

These words of Jesus are introduced here at the very start of this study series because in many ways, Jesus' words capture the main lesson of the book of Daniel. Daniel takes us into an Old Testament time when God's people are facing opposition and pressure to compromise. The book provides the reassurance that allegiance to God will ultimately lead to salvation, because human kingdoms will perish. Irrespective of how important and powerful they may seem now, human empires will eventually fade. But the kingdom of God is everlasting. In this way, Daniel points forward to Jesus Christ—the one who overcame the world and through whom God establishes his kingdom.

Studying the passage

The opening couple of verses of Daniel sound very matter of fact, but behind them lies an unbelievable amount of anxiety, pain and soul searching. The verses describe what is often referred to as 'the Exile'. The Exile occurred about 600 years before Jesus and it resulted from the mighty Babylonian Empire conquering Israel. Babylon swarmed like locusts across the border. Israel's beloved capital city of Jerusalem was destroyed and the precious Temple of

Yahweh[1] reduced to ruins. The Babylonians took Israel's king captive and they carried back to Babylon large numbers of Israelites as prisoners of war (question 1). And there by the waters of Babylon, as captives in a foreign land, the Israelites wept. They wept out of anguish, they wept out of loss and they wept out of confusion (question 2). What had happened? Had Yahweh given up on Israel? Or had the gods of Babylon been too powerful for Yahweh? Either prospect was terrible!

For Israelites like Daniel, the events of the Exile also brought with them a very personal crisis. For starters, they had been torn away from their own homes and families and were now being forced to learn a foreign culture and language. With all this came the challenge of how to live as an Israelite in a foreign land. What do you do when you're now living in a pagan nation instead of an Israelite community? How do you stay true to your identity as an Israelite? Where do you draw the line on particular issues (questions 3-4)? It is here that strong parallels exist between Daniel and the New Testament Christian. Both face the challenge of staying loyal to God in a world which pressures them not to (question 5).

For Daniel this challenge culminates over the issue of eating the king's food. It's interesting to consider why Daniel draws the line on this issue. The text does not fully explain Daniel's actions, but one likely suggestion is that in the ancient near east, sharing a meal with someone was often a sign of dependence and loyalty to them. It was an act that would obligate you towards them. This is what Daniel rejects. Daniel's dependence, loyalty and obligations are with Yahweh the God of Israel, and so he refuses to eat (question 6).

The clear expectation is that Daniel's health will suffer by not eating the king's food. Miraculously, the reverse happens (question 7). The lesson here is that even in tough times, the true man of God stays loyal to God, for, even when trouble and trials occur, God is still sovereign and still in control. This can be seen at numerous points in the chapter. Three times throughout the chapter (vv. 2, 8-9, 17) we are expressly told that God is orchestrating and controlling the events of the chapter. Despite the turmoil of the Exile, God is not absent.

---

1. 'Yahweh'—or as the Hebrew of the Old Testament spells it, 'YHWH'—is God's personal name, revealed to Moses in Exodus 3:13-15. It means "I am who I am" or "I will be who I will be". In most English Bibles, if 'Yahweh' is used in the Hebrew, the English translation 'LORD' is placed in capital letters. Most Jews were careful not to use this name lest they accidentally took God's name in vain. But notice the boldness with which Daniel uses it in Daniel 9!

Indeed, this lesson reaches its climactic point at the very end of the chapter (v. 21): "And Daniel was there until the first year of King Cyrus". King Cyrus was the Persian king who defeated the Babylonians, and so verse 21 carries with it a great encouragement. Daniel, the one who looked like he might get into serious trouble, survived! Meanwhile, Babylon disintegrated around him. The follower of God survived, and the kingdom of Babylon did not (question 8).

To finish

The finishing question is designed to help people reflect on the encouragement of this chapter. It's a chapter that calls on us to have courage and to stand firm in our loyalty to Jesus and his kingdom. No matter how difficult it might be to do that, there will come a time when we will be seen to have done the right thing, for God's kingdom alone will last. In this respect, the finishing question takes us back to Jesus' words from the 'Getting started' question.

2. WISDOM

....

Daniel 2

▶ Remember: 60/40/20

 Getting started

Wisdom is one of the key themes in Daniel 2, so the 'Getting started' question is designed to help stimulate discussion about what exactly wisdom is. Hopefully the discussion will uncover the idea that wisdom is different from knowledge. Wisdom has a practical edge to it. Wisdom is more than simply knowing things; wisdom helps us get through life. The wise person therefore seems to know which decisions and directions to take in order to make the most of this life. This is certainly the way that the Bible describes wisdom.

Studying the passage

The events of the chapter are fairly straightforward. Nebuchadnezzar, the conquering Babylonian king introduced to us in the previous chapter, is troubled by a recurring dream (note the plural in verse 1). In the ancient near east, dreams were commonly seen as the means by which the gods communicated with humans. This would certainly have added to the king's unease (question 1).

Nebuchadnezzar's distress over the dreams is reflected in his command to the wise men of Babylon not only to interpret the dream but to describe the dream as well ... or face death! So seriously does the king view the dream that he wants to make no mistake in understanding it (question 2). The wise men of Babylon are in turn distressed by the king's request and state that, "The thing that the king asks is difficult, and no one can show it to the king except the gods, whose dwelling is not with flesh" (v. 11).

Daniel for his part pleads with God for understanding, and the dream is revealed to him. Daniel praises God and in so doing draws our attention to one of the key themes of the chapter. It is God who shapes life, so ultimately it is only God who can give true wisdom about life (vv. 20-23). It is this truth that Daniel explains to Nebuchadnezzar (vv. 27-28; questions 3-4).

The actual dream of Nebuchadnezzar is eventually described in verses 31-35. In his dream, Nebuchadnezzar sees a statue made of a gold head, silver arms, bronze chest, iron legs and feet which are partly iron and partly clay. However, as imposing as this statue is, a rock appears—cut out not by human hands. This rock breaks the feet of clay and iron and shatters the whole statue. The rock then becomes a mountain that fills the whole earth.

It is revealed to Nebuchadnezzar that he is the head of gold and that the other metals represent different man-made kingdoms that will come after him. It is often suggested that the silver represents the Persian Empire (which conquered the Babylonians), the bronze represents the Greek Empire (which in turned conquered the Persians), and the iron and clay represents the Roman Empire (which in turn conquered the Greeks). This seems a reasonable interpretation. However, the chapter itself makes no such identification, raising the probability that it really doesn't matter (question 6). The main lesson of the dream is not to learn what metals represent which kingdoms. The main lesson of the dream is that they will all be destroyed in the end. It is the kingdom of God that will last forever, as represented by the rock that supernaturally appears, crushes everything and then becomes a mountain that fills the earth (question 7):

> "And in the days of those kings the God of heaven will set up a kingdom that shall never be destroyed, nor shall the kingdom be left to another people. It shall break in pieces all these kingdoms and bring them to an end, and it shall stand forever ..." (v. 44)

This lesson—that the kingdom of God is the *only* kingdom that will endure—is an important one. This lesson was reflected in chapter 1 (see previous study) and it's one that we will return to several times throughout this study series.

After having the dream described and explained to him, Nebuchadnezzar testifies to God as the "God of gods and Lord of kings, and a revealer of mysteries" (question 8; v. 47). This returns us to the key theme of true wisdom coming from God. Question 9 is designed to help pull these threads together.

The words "wisdom" or "wise" are repeatedly used throughout the chapter (vv. 12, 13, 14, 18, 20, 21, 23, 24, 27, 30, 48). We are being shown that the truly wise person understands life from the perspective of God's revelation. In particular, God has revealed that it is his kingdom that will endure forever. The wise person therefore negotiates this life knowing that the kingdom of God is what matters most.

To finish

The finishing question is designed to help people reflect practically on the things we have discovered of God in this chapter. Amongst other things, it's important to see that if it is God who "gives wisdom to the wise and knowledge to those who have understanding" (v. 21), then reading and studying his word is a vital step in living this life. It's also important to note that, since it is the kingdom of God which will endure, the wise person makes Jesus Christ the central priority of his or her lifestyle.

3. SALVATION

Daniel 3 & 6

▶ Remember: 60/40/20

 Getting started

The 'Getting started' question establishes a point of contact between the life of the Christian and the situation for many of the Israelites at the time of Daniel. 1 Peter 2:11 describes the Christians as "sojourners and exiles" in the world. We live in a world that at its best is indifferent and at its worst is violently hostile to Jesus Christ. This is very similar to God's people at the time of the Exile. They too lived in a land and a society in which they were very much the 'odd ones out'. This challenge becomes immediately obvious in chapters 3 and 6.

Studying the passage

The study covers two chapters in which many parallel events occur. In both chapters, God's people are exposed to opposition, victimization and the prospect of a terrible death (the chart in the study will help people notice the details of this in the text). In both chapters, however, God's people remain faithful and are miraculously saved from their punishment. In each case, the story also highlights that the rescue is achieved by divine intervention. In the case of Shadrach, Meshach and Abednego, one "like a son of the gods" appears in the furnace with them, and in the case of Daniel an angel appears to shut the lions' mouths. So compelling are these rescues that in each case the king involved eventually acknowledges the God of Israel (3:28-29, 6:26-27).

Despite these many parallels, the two chapters also have some telling differences. One such difference is the stark difference in personality of the two kings involved. Nebuchadnezzar, the king of Babylon, is far more antagonistic to Shadrach, Meshach and Abednego, whereas Darius, the king of Persia, is more sympathetic and is tricked into having to punish Daniel. The text is showing that, irrespective of the particular empire, the particular king or even the particular type of ruler in power, God's people will inevitably face opposition (question 1).

It is also instructive that in chapter 3, the king's command is for people to actively do something (i.e. bow down to a statue), whereas in chapter 6, the king's command is for people to passively *not* do something (i.e. they are not to pray). The text is highlighting the varied and subtle ways by which the world can work to drive a wedge between God and his people (question 2).

The key lesson of these chapters, however, comes in the fact that Shadrach, Meshach, Abednego and Daniel all remain faithful. Their faithfulness is vindicated by their miraculous rescues. The New Testament urges us all to be spurred on by such men of faith. Their faith helped them to face present hardships for the sake of future glory. This faith is perfected in Jesus Christ,

> ... who for the joy that was set before him endured the cross, despising the shame, and is seated at the right hand of the throne of God.
>
> Consider him who endured from sinners such hostility against himself, so that you may not grow weary or fainthearted. (Heb 12:2-3)

Question 3 provides an opportunity to reflect on Jesus' faith and how it should indeed spur us on. It would also be a good time to return to the words of Jesus quoted at the very beginning of this study series: "In the world you will have tribulation. But take heart; I have overcome the world" (John 16:33).

To finish

Not all of us face the level of opposition that Shadrach, Meshach, Abednego and Daniel did. Nevertheless, many of us still experience degrees of hostility from the world for being a follower of Jesus. This final question is an opportunity for people to share their personal experiences. You may like to talk about the situation of missionaries and other Christians in countries hostile to the gospel.

4. HUMILITY
· ·
Daniel 4-5

▶ Remember: 60/40/20

 Getting started

In this study we again read two chapters that are clearly linked. This time the linking theme is God's rejection of the proud. This is most obviously expressed in 5:18-22.

The 'Getting started' question seeks to raise the issue of pride and its consequences. It is worth pointing out that the saying, "Pride goes before a fall," is in fact drawn from an Old Testament proverb: "Pride goes before destruction, and a haughty spirit before a fall" (Prov 16:18). Other related Proverbs include "The LORD tears down the house of the proud but maintains the widow's boundaries" (Prov 15:25) and "Everyone who is arrogant in heart is an abomination to the LORD; be assured, he will not go unpunished" (Prov 16:5).

Studying the passage

Abraham Lincoln once said, "Nearly all men can stand adversity, but if you want to test a man's character, give him power". Daniel 4 recounts an incident in which power brings out the worst in King Nebuchadnezzar. The chapter takes place at a time in history when Nebuchadnezzar was very, very successful. As the Babylonian Empire grew, Nebuchadnezzar amassed an astronomical amount of wealth, which in turn allowed him to finance many massive building projects. One such project was an impressive palace that became known as the Hanging Gardens of Babylon. It became one of the seven wonders of the ancient world. All this achievement and power causes Nebuchadnezzar to reflect on his own greatness (Dan 4:30; question 1).

Nebuchadnezzar's pride is doubly disappointing (question 2). Not only has he already been warned of pride via a dream (Dan 4:1-27), but our previous studies have shown that Nebuchadnezzar has in fact been convicted of the sovereignty of the God of Israel on more than one occasion (Dan 2:47, 3:28-29). It is a reflection of the insidiousness of pride, that even after such experiences and warnings, Nebuchadnezzar still succumbs to it.

Because of his pride, Nebuchadnezzar is devastatingly humbled:

> Immediately the word was fulfilled against Nebuchadnezzar. He was driven from among men and ate grass like an ox, and his body was wet with the dew of heaven till his hair grew as long as eagles' feathers, and his nails were like birds' claws. (Dan 4:33)

What happened to Nebuchadnezzar is generally considered to be a case of lycanthropy. It is a known condition, though not all that common. It is an emotional breakdown, in which a person becomes delusional and starts to think that he or she is an animal. In the case of Nebuchadnezzar, it's a sobering reminder that it is only by God's sovereign will that anything occurs (question 3).

However, if Nebuchadnezzar's humiliation is stunning, so too is his restoration (question 4). In 4:34-36 we read that Nebuchadnezzar quite literally comes to his senses. He comes to realize that it is only by God's will that we achieve anything in this life, and so his mind is restored. It is in fact a wonderful little account about God's capacity to forgive people. God is always willing to take people back and not hold grudges against them! It is of course an aspect of God that will eventually lead to the coming of Jesus Christ. Jesus came so as to make it possible for the humble to be given grace.

The narrative of Daniel, however, now takes us to a very similar incident but without such a positive ending. In chapter 5, Belshazzar (Nebuchadnezzar's son) also falls victim to pride. Belshazzar's pride shows itself at a banquet when he orders for the goblets that Babylon had ransacked from the Temple in Jerusalem to be brought. These were goblets that were only meant to be used by the Israelite priests in sacrifices to Yahweh at the Jerusalem temple. Yet Belshazzar arrogantly drinks from them and praises the gods of silver and bronze and wood. It is an act of deliberate mockery to the God of Israel. Indeed, it is an act of pride even worse than his father's, for he has failed to learn the lesson of his father (Dan 5:18-22; question 5).

Belshazzar's arrogance results in a hand appearing and mysteriously writing three words on a wall: Mene, Tekel, Peres. Numbered, weighed, divided. The message means that the God whom Belshazzar thought he could ignore has numbered and weighed his life, and Belshazzar has been found lacking. The grim conclusion comes when "that very night Belshazzar the Chaldean king was killed. And Darius the Mede received the kingdom, being about sixty-two years old" (Dan 5:30-31; question 6).

And so the once mighty Babylonian Empire vanishes—all by the hand of God. The lesson of the two chapters is now crystal clear (question 7). It is exactly as Nebuchadnezzar said:

> ... all the inhabitants of the earth are accounted as nothing, and he does according to his will among the host of heaven and among the inhabitants of the earth; and none can stay his hand or say to him, "What have you done?" (Dan 4:35)

This lesson about God's sovereignty and his opposition to pride offers both a comfort and a challenge to God's people. The challenge is that God hates pride and so we should flee from it (question 9). This is a challenge that the New Testament repeats: "Clothe yourselves, all of you, with humility toward one another, for 'God opposes the proud but gives grace to the humble'" (1 Pet 5:5).

The comfort of these chapters, however, can be understood when we remember the context of Daniel. Daniel takes us into a time when Israel is being lauded over by kings and rulers who are so powerful and mighty that they seem untouchable and invincible. But the book of Daniel is showing us that they are not invincible at all! Eventually every human kingdom will vanish and only God's kingdom will endure (see Study 2). Daniel 4-5 reinforces this truth by showing that God does judge the proud powers of this world and they will not go unpunished. God's people therefore ought to press on and stand firm in their faith (question 8).

Jesus himself lived out this lesson. Peter writes of Jesus,

> He committed no sin, neither was deceit found in his mouth. When he was reviled, he did not revile in return; when he suffered, he did not threaten, but continued entrusting himself to him who judges justly. (1 Pet 2:22-23)

Jesus therefore lived the lesson of Daniel 4-5. Jesus was persecuted by proud and arrogant people but he did not retaliate because he knew that there will come a time when God will weigh, measure and divide. So he entrusted himself to him who judges justly (question 10).

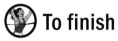 **To finish**

The final question is an opportunity for people to share their personal struggles with pride in their lives.

5. DOMINION

Daniel 7

▶ Remember: 60/40/20

 Getting started

Daniel 7 is a majestic chapter both in its role in the book of Daniel and in the truths that it presents. It is a chapter that provides us with a radical perspective on life. The 'Getting started' question therefore aims to stimulate discussion about what activities we currently think are important in our lives. It's a question that the study will also finish on, so as to help us rethink our answer in the light of what we discover from Daniel 7 (see the 'To finish' question).

Studying the passage

Daniel marks a change in style in the book (question 1). Previously the chapters have been a straightforward narrative in which Daniel has been spoken about in the third person. From Daniel 7 on, however, the chapters change so that Daniel now speaks in the first person about dreams that he personally has. These dreams are particularly full of strange images and symbols. The name given to this style of writing in the Bible is 'apocalyptic'.

Apocalyptic writing can seem confusing. It uses images and vivid word pictures to create a feeling and generate a reaction. In this respect, it is best to be content with the broad feel of an apocalyptic passage rather than get too distracted trying to identify what each and every image represents (if the writer thinks it's important, he will make the identifications for us). Taken in this sense, the vision of Daniel 7 is quite straightforward.

Daniel's vision has three main scenes (question 2). In the first scene, four terrifying beasts come up from a churning, endless sea. There is a lion with wings, a bear with ribs from a fresh kill in its mouth, a leopard with wings and then a fourth beast which is not even likened to any sort of animal. This fourth beast is a picture of savagery and power that is almost unparalleled. It is so terrible that there is nothing to even compare it to!

The scene then changes to the throne room of the Ancient of Days. God himself in blinding white and flaming fire sets up his throne in front of the four beasts. The mood is now one of anticipation. The reader is expecting a cosmic conflict to explode between God and the terrible beasts. There is, however, no battle scene at all! Despite how fierce and powerful the beasts seem, even the fourth one is swept aside.

It is then that a third, very surprising scene occurs. One "like a son of man" (i.e. a normal looking person) is given all the power and authority by God. Despite how fierce and intimidating the beasts are, it is not they who have the dominion at all!

It is revealed to Daniel that the beasts in fact represent man-made kingdoms (Dan 7:17; question 3). It is understandable therefore that many people spend lots of time trying to determine which specific kingdoms the four beasts represent. Parallels between Daniel's dream and Nebuchadnezzar's dream in chapter 2 have meant that a common explanation is that the beasts represent the Babylonian, Persian, Greek and Roman Empires. According to this interpretation, the boastful horn of the fourth beast corresponds to Antiochus Epiphanes, a particularly vicious persecutor of God's people in history. This seems a likely interpretation, however the chapter itself does not explicitly say so. The main focus of the chapter is not on the beasts but on the "one like a son of man".

Within the chapter, the "one like a son of man" is identified as a symbol for the "saints of the Most High", since they are the ones who are given sovereignty and power over the kingdoms under heaven (vv. 17-18, 21-22, 27; question 4). This would have been a great comfort for God's people at the time of Daniel. Struggling as they were under oppressive tyrants and empires, this dream assured them of the hope that, in time, all kingdoms will be swept aside and eventually sovereignty and power will be granted to God's people (question 5). This is a pivotal lesson in the book of Daniel, for it gives us an explanation for the events of the previous chapters. This is why Shadrach, Meshach and Abednego would not bow to the statue of Nebuchadnezzar (chapter 3) and why Daniel was prepared to refuse the king's food (chapter 1) and be thrown to the lions for praying (chapter 6). These men saw life from the perspective of Daniel's vision. They courageously lived out the truth that "the kingdom and the dominion and the greatness of the kingdoms under the whole heaven shall be given to the people of the saints of the Most High" (Dan 7:27).

When we turn to the New Testament, however, Jesus does something very radical. By referring to himself as the Son of Man (e.g. Mark 14:60-62), Jesus identifies himself as the true Israel, a person of everlasting dominion that will never fade. His is a kingdom that will endure forever (questions 6-7). Daniel 7 therefore provides us with a truly majestic picture of what things really matter most in life. Despite what the world might say and promote as being important, it is the things to do with Jesus that matter most.

This is an invigorating and exciting lesson that can transform even the seemingly mundane things of life. Reading the Bible with our children, a word of comfort to a Christian friend, lending someone a Christian book to read, standing out as a Christian at school, giving encouragement at our Bible study group, helping behind the scenes at a youth group, struggling with a Scripture class, spending time in prayer or with people—these are all things that we can tend to overlook and not see the true value of. But according to Daniel 7 they are the things that will probably have more eternal significance than most of the other apparently bigger things that fill our lives. For these are things that contribute to the kingdom of the Son of Man, a kingdom that will endure when all else fades.

 To finish

The final question is an opportunity for people to consider whether their personal lifestyle goals and value systems reflect the perspective on life in Daniel 7.

6. ENDURANCE

Daniel 8

▶ Remember: 60/40/20

 ## Getting started

The persecution of God's people has already appeared as a major theme within Daniel (see chapters 1, 3 and 6). This theme is again revisited in Daniel 8, only now from the perspective of a warning about future persecution, rather than the retelling of past persecution. The 'Getting started' question invites people to consider how to help support someone who is being worn down by the opposition of the world.

Studying the passage

Daniel 8 continues in the style of the previous chapter. Daniel again informs us of a disturbing vision which he received. Again the vision is first recounted (vv. 1-14) and then its interpretation given (vv. 15-27).

The vision centres on the appearance of a ram and a goat (questions 1-3). The ram is the first to appear and he is fierce and powerful: "No beast could stand before him, and there was no one who could rescue from his power" (v. 4). Despite the ram's apparent invincibility, a goat charges from the west and tramples the ram underfoot. Afterwards, considerable detail is given to the growth of various horns on the goat. This loss of power by the ram and then the succession of horns, some of which are broken off at the height of their power (v. 8), creates a mood of struggle and confusion. The world is full of battles and power struggles but irrespective of how invincible something may seem at the time, its dominion and success is always fleeting.

The interpretation of the vision reveals that the ram represents the Empire of the Medes and Persians (v. 20), whereas the goat represents the Greek Empire (v. 21).

Given this interpretation from the text, we can now see that Daniel's vision provides a good overview of the history of the Greek Empire. Under the leadership of Alexander the Great (v. 21), the Greek Empire grew greatly in size and power. After Alexander's early death, however, the Empire was divided amongst four of his generals who jostled each other for power (vv. 22-23; questions 4-5).

Within the chapter, one particular horn of the goat is given considerable attention (vv. 9-12). The interest in this horn is because it is responsible for opposition to and persecution of God's people (vv. 11-12). It is generally considered that the "king of bold face" is a reference to Antiochus Epiphanes. Epiphanes was a particularly vicious persecutor of God's people and, amongst other things, banned Sabbath-keeping and circumcision amongst the Israelites, violently punished those who disobeyed him, and set up sacrifices to his god in the Jerusalem temple (question 6).

As troubling as the vision is, comfort is found in the fact that ultimately the persecutor of God's people will be destroyed (v. 25; question 7). The lesson for God's people is to endure. Opposition will come to an end in God's timing. In this respect, Daniel 8 continues to build on the lesson of the previous study. Ultimately it is God's kingdom, the kingdom of the Son of Man, which will endure and last for ever. God's people are therefore called on to persevere (question 8). Even within the midst of violent opposition to his name, God has not lost control. This lesson is especially seen in the life, death and resurrection of Jesus Christ. Even at the hideous point of Jesus' crucifixion, the greatest evil that humanity could produce, God was ingeniously bringing about his purposes (question 9).

 To finish

Daniel 8 encourages God's people to persevere by warning them of a future hardship, and reminding them that God will not lose control during it. Hardships will eventually come to an end. The final question invites people to share other biblical truths and passages that help them endure.

7. FORGIVENESS

Daniel 9

▶ Remember: 60/40/20

 ## Getting started

God is often perceived as a cosmic grumpy old man who is quick to find fault with people. Such a terrible misrepresentation of God comes in part from:

a) a failure to appreciate the offensiveness of our sin; and

b) a failure to appreciate the amazing love, patience and forbearance of God.

These issues are raised for discussion in the opening question because Daniel 9 provides a wonderful Old Testament opportunity to see that God's natural disposition is to show love: "But you, O Lord, are a God merciful and gracious, slow to anger and abounding in steadfast love and faithfulness" (Ps 86:15).

Studying the passage

The opening verses of Daniel 9 are tingling with anticipation for two main reasons. Firstly, it is the first year of Darius' reign. Darius was the king of the Median and Persian Empire that conquered the Babylonians. This change in the political landscape raised the possibility of Israel's Exile ending. Babylon is now no more! Maybe the Persians would even release Israel and let them go home?

A second reason for this hope is that the prophet Jeremiah had predicted that the Exile would end after 70 years (questions 1-2). The first year of Darius (v. 1) places this chapter about 65-70 years after the start of the Exile! This must have filled Daniel with a strong hope that the Exile was coming to an end. Prompted by this anticipation, Daniel is moved to prayer (question 3). As such, Daniel does exactly what Jeremiah had said to do:

"Then you will call upon me and come and pray to me, and I will hear you. You will seek me and find me. When you seek me with all your heart, I will be found by you, declares the LORD, and I will restore your fortunes and gather you from all the nations and all the places where I have driven you, declares the LORD, and I will bring you back to the place from which I sent you into exile." (Jer 29:12-14)

Daniel's prayer is one of deep confession. He admits that the Exile was Israel's own fault. The Exile was a just punishment from God because of their wickedness (question 4):

All Israel has transgressed your law and turned aside, refusing to obey your voice. And the curse and oath that are written in the Law of Moses the servant of God have been poured out upon us, because we have sinned against him. (Dan 9:11)

Following his confession of sin, Daniel asks God to forgive and restore his people. It is noteworthy that Daniel begs for God to act this way, not because they deserve it, but because God himself is merciful (questions 5-6).

Now therefore, O our God, listen to the prayer of your servant and to his pleas for mercy, and for your own sake, O Lord, make your face to shine upon your sanctuary, which is desolate. O my God, incline your ear and hear. Open your eyes and see our desolations, and the city that is called by your name. For we do not present our pleas before you because of our righteousness, but because of your great mercy. (Dan 9: 17-18)

We can learn much from Daniel. In many ways he is the classic example of how to approach God. We approach him on our hands and knees begging for mercy, for all of us are unworthy and guilty of sin. To casually approach God as if we're on equal terms with him shows a level of arrogance and impertinence that will bring very serious consequences (see Study 4).

One of the truly wonderful insights of this chapter is the eagerness with which God responds to Daniel's prayer (question 8). Before Daniel even has a chance to finish his prayer, God's answer is on the way (vv. 20, 23). Indeed, it is a measure of how keen God is to show forgiveness that he now provides Daniel with an overview into his plan for forgiveness (v. 24).

The final four verses of the chapter, in which God gives Daniel an overview for his plan to provide "everlasting righteousness" for his people, are quite difficult. Many people have used these verses to develop elaborate timelines for either the first appearance of Jesus or the return of Jesus. The verses, however, seem to be deliberately vague. Rather than giving a highly detailed plan to Daniel, God instead simply wants Daniel to know that a plan exists. Rather than Daniel knowing exactly who each anointed person is, God simply wants Daniel to know that anointed people do exist and that at the right time, people will be raised up, events will happen and in God's good timing everything will be brought to completion. At just the right time, sin will be put to an end, wickedness will be atoned for and everlasting righteousness will be ushered in (question 9).

This side of the cross we can see that God's plan to bring in everlasting righteousness is wonderfully fulfilled in Christ. Through Christ's death and resurrection, God's people have been washed clean of sin forever. We enjoy the astounding blessing of everlasting righteousness before God (question 10). This blessing is all the more staggering given the preciousness of Jesus' sacrifice:

> In this the love of God was made manifest among us, that God sent his only Son into the world, so that we might live through him. (1 John 4:9)

 ## To finish

Sometimes when life is hard we can forget just how good God is. The final question is designed to help people personally reflect on the characteristics of God revealed in this chapter—God's enthusiasm to forgive, his eagerness to restore and his commitment to bring in everlasting righteousness through Jesus Christ.

8. HOPE

....

Daniel 10-12

▶ Remember: 60/40/20

 ## Getting started

The final three chapters of Daniel are the most complex and challenging of the book. Chapters 10-12 describe a single revelation that describes "what is to happen to your people [i.e. Israel] in the latter days. For the vision is for days yet to come" (10:14). Most commentators observe that many of the details within the vision bear a strong parallel to events during the Greek Empire when Israel underwent a fierce persecution. In this respect, the Matthias Media Interactive Bible Study on Daniel (*Kingdom of Dreams*) has a helpful summary of the vision. The summary has been reproduced at the end of the study (see pp. 42-43).

For the purposes of this study, however, we will be content to simply grasp some of the main ideas and not be too distracted with detail (much of which is very hard to fully understand). In this respect, the main lesson of the chapters is that, despite the future trials that await them, God has not lost control and blessing awaits those who endure to the end (12:1-2). The main pastoral concern of the vision is therefore to provide hope and reassurance to God's people. It is this theme of hope which the 'Getting started' question seeks to raise, by asking people to consider some of the difficulties of remaining convinced that God is in control in their own life.

Studying the passage

Chapter 10 is mainly concerned with a description of the messenger who brings the vision to Daniel. Daniel is told that the message concerns a future war that will engulf his people (question 1). It would seem that this war will involve the Empires of both Persia and Greece (question 3). Daniel has been chosen as the recipient of the vision because of his humble desire to gain understanding. This recaptures some of the lessons of previous chapters, in which we have discovered that a wise understanding of life comes only from God (question 2). As Daniel himself has said,

"Blessed be the name of God forever and ever, to whom belong wisdom and might. He changes times and seasons; he removes kings and sets up kings; he gives wisdom to the wise and knowledge to those who have understanding ..." (Dan 2:20-21)

As the vision unfolds in chapter 11, quite precise predictions of political intrigue and struggle seem to be made. Many of these can be linked to known historical events (see the summary on pages 42-43). The effect of reading about the nature of this struggle produces feelings of confusion, and even despair, within the reader. God's people seem to be at the mercy of political powers far mightier than they. They seem to be tossed to and fro by powerful empires and individuals (question 4). The comfort of the vision, however, comes in the recurring theme that, although complex, the events of the vision occur at "appointed" times. Despite the apparent confusion of events, they are in fact occurring under God's sovereign control (question 5). It is again as Daniel has said above:

"Blessed be the name of God forever and ever, to whom belong wisdom and might. He changes times and seasons; *he removes kings and sets up kings* ..." (Dan 2:20-21)

The details of chapter 12 are again hard to fully understand. Some think it is another reference to the fierce persecution of God's people under Antiochus Epiphanes (see Study 6). Others think that the vision has now jumped forward to a future persecution that will happen just before the return of Jesus. Irrespective of these options, there is comfort in the truth that God's people will ultimately be delivered. The wise and faithful who have persevered to the end will be raised to everlasting life. They will shine like stars forever and ever (question 6). By contrast, those who are not God's own will awake to everlasting shame and contempt (question 7).

The implications of this truth are enormous. Throughout all areas of life, the wise person of God understands that the most important thing is to persevere in their faith. Everything that hinders and jeopardizes this must be thrown off (Heb 12:1). Question 8 encourages us to explore some of the areas of life that might be affected by this truth.

🧑 To finish

The finishing question asks people to review some of the ways in which Daniel has helped us to see the things of this world from God's perspective. Hopefully this will also provide an opportunity to see how these truths are also expressed in Jesus. Some examples of this are:

- Daniel has repeatedly shown us that the kingdoms of man will eventually fade and perish (e.g. Studies 2, 5). The kingdom of God will alone last. This lesson points forward to Jesus, the one through whom God establishes his kingdom.

- Daniel has repeatedly shown us that the wise person of God understands that God's kingdom lasts forever and therefore refuses to compromise their loyalty to God (e.g. Studies 1, 3). Jesus himself exemplified this (Heb 12:2).

- Daniel has repeatedly shown us that God never loses control of events, even when those events may seem terrible (e.g. Studies 6, 8). The cross of Christ exemplifies this most graphically.

- Daniel has repeatedly shown us that God opposes the proud but brings forgiveness to the repentant and the humble (e.g. Studies 4, 7). This attribute of God again points us forward to Jesus, the one through whom God brings forgiveness to the humble.

Matthias Media is a ministry team of like-minded, evangelical Christians working together to achieve a particular goal, as summarized in our mission statement:

> *To serve our Lord Jesus Christ, and the growth of his gospel in the world, by producing and delivering high quality, Bible-based resources.*

It was in 1988 that we first started pursuing this mission together, and in God's kindness we now have more than 250 different ministry resources being distributed all over the world. These resources range from Bible studies and books, through to training courses and audio sermons.

To find out more about our large range of very useful products, and to access samples and free downloads, visit our website:

www.matthiasmedia.com.au

How to purchase our resources

1 Through a range of outlets in various parts of the world: visit **www.matthiasmedia.com.au/international.php** for details about recommended retailers in your part of the world.

2 Direct from us over the internet:
 – in the US: www.matthiasmedia.com
 – in Australia and the rest of the world: www.matthiasmedia.com.au

3 Direct from us by phone:
 – within Australia: 1800 814 360 (Sydney: 9663 1478)
 – international: +61-2-9663-1478

4 Trade enquiries worldwide:
 – email us: sales@matthiasmedia.com.au

More Pathway Bible Guides

Pathway Bible Guides are simple, straightforward easy-to-read Bible studies, ideal for:

- people who are new to studying the Bible;
- groups with limited time for study.

We've designed the studies to be short and easy to use, with an uncomplicated vocabulary. At the same time, we've tried to do justice to the passages being studied, and to model good Bible-reading principles. Pathway Bible Guides are simple without being simplistic; no-nonsense without being no-content.

Beginning with God
Genesis 1-12

Getting to Know God
Exodus 1-20

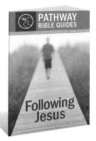

Following Jesus
Luke 9-12

Peace with God
Romans

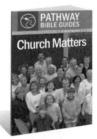

Church Matters
1 Corinthians 1-7

Standing Firm
1 Thessalonians

FOR MORE INFORMATION OR TO ORDER CONTACT:

Matthias Media
Telephone: +61-2-9663-1478 | Facsimile: +61-2-9663-3265
Email: sales@matthiasmedia.com.au

www.matthiasmedia.com.au